Grand-Mommy and Me

Elizabeth Braziel Banks

WestBow Press books may be ordered through booksellers or by contacting:

WestBow Press
A Division of Thomas Nelson & Zondervan
1663 Liberty Drive
Bloomington, IN 47403
www.westbowpress.com
844-714-3454

ISBN: 978-1-5127-4141-4 (sc)
ISBN: 978-1-5127-4142-1 (e)

Library of Congress Control Number: 2016907448

Print information available on the last page.

WestBow Press rev. date: 12/09/2020

WestBow
PRESS®
A DIVISION OF THOMAS NELSON
& ZONDERVAN

This book is dedicated to my adorable grandchildren,
Marcus Jr., Kaira Elizabeth and Meilani Lynna.
Grand-Mommy loves you so very much!

About the Author

Elizabeth Braziel Banks was inspired to write Grand-Mommy and Me when her first grandchild was born. She earned a Master of Arts Degree in Higher Education and has had an interest in writing plays and children's literature for many years. She is a graduate of the Institute of Children's Literature and a member of the Society of Children's Book Writers and Illustrators. She lives in San Antonio, Texas.

I love my grand-mommy,
And my grand-mommy loves me.
She says I'm her blessing you see.

Grand-Mommy knows just how to make me laugh,
Even when I'm taking a bath.

She teaches me all sorts of things,
Like letters and numbers and colors that bling.

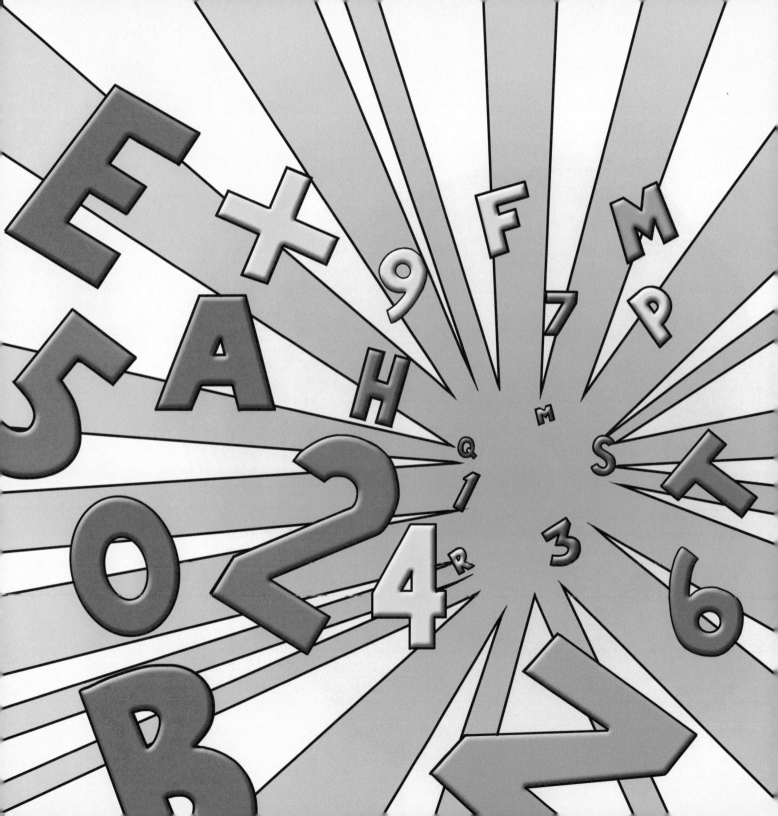

My grand-mommy plays
"This Little Piggy"

with my toes.

She likes to kiss me on my nose,
And dress me in my favorite clothes.

She reads my favorite story of Pooh.
I get tickled when we play "Peek a Boo".

Grand-Mommy sometimes takes me to the...

When I fret and don't want to sleep,
She looks into my room and takes a peek.

Into her arms I go with a leap.

Then she knows just what to do.
She says, "I'll sing a song for you."

"Grand-Mommy loves that baby.
Oh, she loves that baby.
Mmm, she loves that baby,
Loves that baby, yes.

Grand-Mommy's gonna sing to the baby.
Oh, she's gonna sing to the baby.
Mmm, she's gonna sing to the baby,
Sing to the baby, yes.

Grand-Mommy's gonna
dance with the baby.
Oh, she's gonna dance with the baby.
Mmm, she's gonna dance with the baby,
Dance with the baby, yes.

Grand-Mommy's gonna rock that baby.
Oh, she's gonna rock that baby.
Mmm, she's gonna rock that baby,
Rock that baby, yes."

GRAND-MOMMY LOVES THAT BABY

Grand - Mom - my loves that ba - by. Oh, she loves that ba - by

Mmm, she loves that ba - by, loves that ba - by yes.

Grand - Mom - my's gon - na sing to the ba - by. Oh,

she's gon - na sing to the ba - by. Mmm, she's gon - na sing

to the ba - by sing to the ba - by, yes.

Printed in the United States
By Bookmasters